Starting a Voluntary Group

THE LEGAL CHOICES

D1824366

The National Council for Voluntary Organisations provides professional advisory services to voluntary organisations, protects their interests and promotes new forms of social action.

Other titles in the NCVO Practical Guides series:

Employing People in Voluntary Organisations
Evaluation in Voluntary Organisations
Finding and Running Premises
Government Grants: A guide for voluntary organisations
Organising Your Finances (forthcoming)
Voluntary Organisations and the Media

Starting a Voluntary Group

THE LEGAL CHOICES

SALLY CAPPER

AN NCVO PRACTICAL GUIDE

BEDFORD SQUARE PRESS | NCVO

Published by
BEDFORD SQUARE PRESS of the
National Council for Voluntary Organisations
26 Bedford Square, London WC1B 3HU

© NCVO 1987

ISBN 0 7199 1180 X

First published 1987

Typeset by D. P. Media Limited, Hitchin, Hertfordshire

Printed and bound in England by
Henry Ling Ltd at the
Dorset Press, Dorchester, Dorset

Contents

Acknowledgements
The author would like to thank the following people: John Edginton and Susan Bates, the authors of *Legal Structures for Voluntary Organisations*, on which this text was based; Adrian Longley, Legal Adviser to NCVO, who gave advice on the text and wrote the Postscript; and Trish Gibson.

1 Introduction

When starting a voluntary group, members are not required by law to establish it in any particular way. It may be possible for your project to achieve its aims without a written document. However, basing the operation purely on verbal agreement can lead to difficulties. Members may disagree as to the aims of the project or how it should be controlled and run, particularly once the founder members have left. A formal legal framework provides a reference point for members and a means of resolving disputes. It gives a group an identity, a measure of continuity and credibility when looking for finance.

Putting it in writing – the governing instrument

'Governing instrument' is a comprehensive term for the document or documents which provide the framework of rules for an organisation.

It will probably be called something else – a constitution, trust deed, or memoran-dum and articles of association – depending on which kind of legal body the group chooses to become.

The drafting of a governing instrument is all important, not only because it will regulate the future running of the group, but because there may be specific legal requirements to be satisfied, e.g. if you wish to be accepted as a charity (see chapter 3). It is often prudent to seek legal advice in its preparation.

However, many organisations produce specimen or model documents which have been prepared with legal advice and you may be able to make use of a suitable one for your group. If there is a parent body for your kind of organisation then it is best to approach it and find out if a model document is available. (See the appendix, p. 00 for a list of groups that produce model documents.) The Charity Commission also have available a list of organisations that produce model documents whose objects clause they have accepted.

Great care should be taken in substantially altering or adapting a model document without legal advice. However, it is generally made clear where variations are possible.

Choosing a legal structure

The law recognises several different ways of organising a project to each of which different rules apply. Each legal structure (or constitutional form) allows you to do certain things, but prohibits or makes it difficult to do others. You will want to choose the one which is best suited not only to achieve the aims of your project but to enable you to run it the way you want.

Once you have worked out the aims of the group (known as its 'objects' and set out in the 'objects clause' of the governing instrument), and the means by which it is intended to achieve them, ask yourselves the following questions:

- Who is to have the final say: the group itself or a wider membership?
- Will the group need to own buildings or other property?
- Will the group need to involve workers in decision making on a democratic basis?
- Is the group likely to change its mind about the running of the project in the near future?
- Will the group be working on a low or reasonably high budget?
- Are substantial contracts (including contracts of employment) likely to be involved so that an individual member of the group might be unwilling or ill-advised to accept personal liability?

The answers to these questions should assist you in making your decision. It might be helpful also to talk to people in projects similar to your own to find out why they adopted the structure they have and if this structure causes them any problems.

The three basic constitutional forms to be considered in this guide are:

- an unincorporated association
- a trust
- a limited company

Two special types – the friendly society and the industrial and provident society – are also discussed. The unincorporated association, trust and friendly society are all unincorporated. The limited company and industrial and provident society are incorporated.

When a group is incorporated it becomes something more than the sum of its members. It attains separate legal identity and can own property, enter into contracts and become legally liable just as an individual can. Incorporation of a group offers to an individual acting on its behalf some protection from liability in contract or tort (civil wrong).

Choosing to become a charity

Charitable status can be of great advantage to a group. It is not dependent on constitutional form or legal structure so that any of the legal bodies listed above and considered below may be charities. They do, however, have to fulfil other requirements and these are dealt with in chapter 3.

2 Legal Structures

The simplest form of legal structure is the unincorporated association. Its governing instrument is generally called a constitution but the document may just be called society or club rules.

What it means

'Unincorporated' means that the organisation has no identity in law except as a collection of individuals. Any one of these individuals acting on behalf of the association can be personally liable for any debts incurred (see below).

What it can do

An unincorporated association can

- have full choice in appointing officers and committee members
- easily dissolve itself or amend its constitution at a general meeting. (There are restrictions on amending the objects clause of a charity, however. See chapter 3)

What it cannot do

An unincorporated association cannot

- hold property without appointing trustees to do so on its behalf
- take legal action, borrow money or enter into any form of contract in its own name but can only do so in the name of one or more individuals

Advantages

- It is cheap to set up. Unlike some of the other structures there are no fees to pay (unless you seek advice from a solicitor).
- It can be set up quickly. You do not have to involve any other organisations (unless you are seeking registration as a charity. See chapter 3).
- It is flexible. It can suit a wide variety of groups, objects and ways of working.
- It is not subject to interference. Some other legal structures are answerable to a statutory authority (an unincorporated association that is also a charity is subject to supervision by the Charity Commissioners, however).

3

Disadvantages

- It cannot hold property in its own name. There must be trustees to hold it in their own names on behalf of the association.
- Members or officers who incur debts on behalf of the association are personally liable for these debts
  Example. An unincorporated association buys an electric typewriter on hire purchase and then finds it cannot keep up the payments. Whoever signed the hire purchase agreement on behalf of the group is legally responsible for paying off the debt.
- The lack of control from an outside body leaves an organisation vulnerable if there is a dispute between members. A friendly society can refer a dispute to the Registrar of Friendly Societies. The small fee charged may be much cheaper than seeking legal advice which an unincorporated association not registered under the Friendly Societies Act might have to do.
- It is difficult to borrow money. Money will only be lent to members of the managing committee as individuals who will be personally responsible for its repayments even though it has been used exclusively to finance the association.

So if your group

- is small
- has a limited and specific purpose
- operates on a low budget
- does not need to own property or employ staff
- wants participation by its membership (from whom the management committee will be drawn)

an unincorporated association may be right for you.

The trust

If your organisation wishes to own property or employ staff *and* is capable of being a charity (see page 10) you may wish to establish a trust. For technical legal reasons a trust is not a suitable structure for a voluntary organisation which is not also a charity, so your group will have to satisfy the requirements of charitable status (see chapter 3) before this choice is available.

The governing instrument of a trust is usually a trust deed.

What it means

A trust is a structure where land or other property including money is held and managed for clearly defined purposes. It creates a relationship between three parties – the donors of the property or money, the trustees in whom the property is vested and the beneficiaries.

Example. A house is given by a benefactor to provide a day nursery. The trustees become the owners of the house but run it as directed in the trust deed for the benefit of local children and their parents. Although the trustees become the nominal owners of the trust property, they have a duty not to profit personally from it in any way. This duty is strictly enforced and extends to prohibition on purchasing trust property even at a fair price. The trustees will be legally liable for this or any other breach of trust including one arising from negligence. There is, however, a power for the court to relieve a trustee from personal liability where he or she has acted honestly and reasonably and ought fairly to be excused for a breach of trust.

What it can do

A trust can

- hold property
- raise funds for the objects of the organisation stated in the trust deed

What it cannot do

- easily remove trustees

Advantages

- It can be set up quickly and fairly cheaply (but you are more likely to need legal advice to prepare a trust deed than to prepare the constitution of an unincorporated association).

4

- It can be cheap to run. Trustees must keep proper accounts and, if the trust is a *registered* charity, must submit them as required to the Charity Commissioners. However, these obligations are less onerous than those required of a company limited by guarantee under the Companies Act 1985.
- A trust deed can be easily amended provided that provision for amendment is made in the original trust deed. A deed which permits the objects clause to be amended, however, will not be acceptable to the Charity Commissioners (see chapter 3).
- A trust is free from direct interference from outside authorities save that as a charity it will be subject to the overall supervision of the Charity Commissioners.

Disadvantages
- The type of management structure it imposes is undemocratic and probably unsuitable for a group which wants participation of a large membership in decision making.
- The power lies with the trustees. Unlike a company where ultimately the members can remove the directors if they do not act in accordance with their wishes, there is no such democratic method for removing the trustees of a trust. So if, for example, the people working for a trust do not think that its trustees are using their power effectively, they have no authority to compel the trustees to mend their ways. Since removal of trustees is difficult and trustees are not usually appointed for a fixed term of office but are there until they resign, are removed or die, such differences of opinion can be difficult to resolve. It is possible within the framework of a trust to reduce the possibility of this type of conflict arising by allowing workers to attend meetings of the trustees.
- Trustees are personally liable to the trust for any loss resulting from their actions which are in breach of trust.

- Because a trust is unincorporated, trustees will be personally liable for contracts they enter into on behalf of a trust. They will, however, be entitled to reimbursement from trust funds. In theory they can protect themselves by not entering into any contract unless their liability is limited to the extent of the trust funds. Difficult to achieve in practice, this calls for the help of a solicitor.
- Transferring property to new trustees can be troublesome and expensive.

To sum up
A trust may be the right legal structure for your group
- if you are capable of being a charity (see page 10)
- if your aim is to raise funds for a specific purpose or run a project with limited objectives
- if you want to adopt a formal structure quickly and cheaply
- if your organisation wishes to own property
- if you do not require the active participation of a large membership

The trust in a minor role

This chapter has dealt with the trust as the legal structure of a group or organisation. However, the trust can also be used in a subsidiary role.

Where an unincorporated association wishes to own property, its members may appoint persons as trustees who will hold the property in their names on behalf of the association. Where trustees of this kind have no managerial functions whatsoever they are known as 'holding trustees'. (See 'Official Custodian for Charities' (page 13) in whom property may be vested on behalf of a charity.) 'Charity trustees' on the other hand – for example, the committee of an unincorporated association – may have managerial but no holding functions. (See chapter 3.)

The friendly society

What it means

Strictly a friendly society is an unincorporated association formed to provide insurance benefits for its members. However, the term is often extended to include other unincorporated associations which are permitted to register under the Friendly Societies Act 1974. These include societies formed for any benevolent or charitable purpose.

To qualify for registration in this category, the purpose of the society must be to benefit persons other than the members themselves or their families. Although such societies may be charitable if they fulfil the necessary criteria (see chapter 3), they need not be so. The society must have a minimum of 7 members and a registered office.

What it can do

A friendly society can

- hold property through trustees
- convert into a company

If a friendly society has charitable objects (see chapter 3) and registers with the Registrar of Friendly Societies, it is exempt from the requirement to register with the Charity Commissioners.

Advantages

- The friendly society like any other unincorporated association needs trustees to hold any property on its behalf. However, on the death, resignation or removal of a trustee all property held in his or her name automatically passes to the succeeding trustee(s). This avoids the trouble and legal expense of conveyances on each occasion.
- There is cheap arbitration in the case of disputes through the Registrar of Friendly Societies (£35 at May 1986).
- Friendly societies can amalgamate easily.

Disadvantages

- The privacy enjoyed by unincorporated associations disappears when an organisation registers under the Friendly Societies Act. There is provision for copies of the rules and the last balance sheet to be made public.
- There are strict requirements for annual accounts and audit. Regular valuation of assets must be sent to the Registrar.
- The contents of the rules (though not their detail) must be as specified by the Friendly Societies Act.
- The freedom from interference from outside authorities also disappears. The Registrar has the power to investigate the affairs of the society and can prohibit the society from accepting new members if it is thought that the circumstances warrant this.

To sum up

Registration under the Friendly Societies Act may be right for you

- if you wish to remain unincorporated
- if you welcome the discipline of some external rules together with a facility to solve disputes without great expense
- if you anticipate transferring property between trustees and want to avoid expensive legal fees

The company limited by guarantee

If your organisation seeks a democratic form of control, has a fairly substantial budget and the members of the management committee wish to minimise the risk of personal loss, then you should consider registering as a company limited by guarantee.

What it means

The company limited by guarantee is a corporate body – that is it has a legal identity of its own apart from its members.

In this it resembles the type of limited company more usually encountered, the company limited by shares. The members of a company limited by shares invest money in the company by buying shares in the hope of making a profit. Their liability is limited to the value of their individual shareholdings. This structure is not suitable for a voluntary group whose incentive to participate will be not profit but commitment to the objects of the organisation.

In the company limited by guarantee, each member's liability is limited to a nominal sum – usually not more than £5, which he or she guarantees to pay if the company has debts on winding up.

A limited company must submit its governing instrument to the Registrar of Companies. The governing instrument consists of two parts:

- *memorandum of association* which states the objects of the organisation, the powers the company has to pursue its objects and the extent of the liability of the members on winding up
- *articles of association* which set out the rules by which the company is to be run, including proceedings at meetings, voting procedures, accounting procedures and the method of electing the management committee (often referred to as the board of directors)

What it can do

A company limited by guarantee can

- hold property without appointing trustees to do so on its behalf
- enter into contracts and take legal action in its own name

Advantages

- Owning and transferring property is simplified. Not only do no trustees have to be appointed as nominal owners, but since a company has no natural life span it can continue to hold property so long as it is in existence. This avoids the trouble and legal expenses of regular conveyances.
- The company is liable for its own debts so that the personal property of the members is not put at risk.
- A company undertakes all its activities in its own right, including taking legal action.
- A democratic structure is provided – the members elect the directors (management committee) and have the right to remove them.
- Regulations made under the Companies Act 1985 provide a ready-made constitution easily adaptable to meet the needs of different groups.
- The company framework is suitable for any size of organisation, so a small organisation can expand without being restricted by the structure it has adopted.
- It is usually easier for an incorporated organisation to borrow money: the lender has the security of the company's assets.
- Only two people are needed to form a company. A friendly society and an industrial and provident society require a minimum of seven members.

Disadvantages

- A company limited by guarantee is subject to more controls than any of the other legal structures.
- There is a lack of privacy. Information on a company's activities is submitted to the Registrar of Companies and is available for public scrutiny.
- The initial and running costs can be high, including
  - a registration fee (£50 at May 1986)
  - legal fees to a solicitor for assistance in establishing the company
  - a recurring fee for submitting annual returns
  - recurring administrative costs, including auditing fees, through having to comply with the Companies Act(s).

To sum up

- The ostensible advantages of incorporation must be set against the inescapable initial and running expenses, so that if you are a group with a small budget and little or no property, becoming a company limited by guarantee is probably not worthwhile.
- If your organisation employs staff, holds property and is feeling inhibited by its unincorporated status, then you should certainly consider becoming a company

limited by guarantee – but first look at what an industrial and provident society can offer.

The industrial and provident society

If your organisation requires the benefits of incorporation without the expense and complexity of a limited company, then you should consider whether to register as an industrial and provident society (IPS).

What it means
An organisation qualifies for registration as an IPS if it is a society for carrying on an industry, business or trade and is either a bona-fide co-operative society *or* is intended to be conducted for the benefit of the community *and* there are special reasons why it should be registered as an IPS rather than under the Companies Acts.

Registration is with the Registrar of Friendly Societies – under the Industrial and Provident Societies Act 1965.

The Act does not define what a 'bona-fide co-operative society' is but the Registrar of Friendly Societies has issued guidelines. To summarise these, in a bona-fide co-operative society

- business must be conducted for the mutual benefit of its members in such a way that the benefit obtained will stem from members participation in its business
- all members will have an equal say in the running of the society – 'one man one vote'
- interest on share and loan capital will be at a moderate rate
- if the society makes a profit after payment of interest on share capital, it will be distributable to members to the extent to which they have traded with or taken part in the business of the society. This could be as a dividend paid on purchases from the co-operative (co-operative shops pay dividends to their customers), or as a bonus paid to workers on sales to the co-operative.

In some societies, e.g. social clubs, profits should not be distributed among members but ploughed back to lessen the cost of or improve the amenities available to members.

- there should be no artificial restriction on membership to increase the value of members' rights (size of premises, etc. may restrict membership in practice)

The Registrar's guidelines for an organisation 'for the benefit of the community' in summary provide that such a society must show that it will benefit persons other than its own members and that its business will be in the interests of the community.

The Registrar also has regard to whether it

- is non profit-making
- is prohibited by its rules from distributing its assets among members
- gives each member an equal say in the running of the society (one man, one vote)
- pays only moderate interest on share and loan capital
- has no artificial restriction on membership

What it can do
An industrial and provident society can

- own property in its own right
- convert to a company limited by guarantee if required using a simplified procedure

If an IPS has charitable objects (see chapter 3), registration with the Registrar of Friendly Societies will exempt it from the requirement to register with the Charity Commissioners.

Advantages
- The benefits of incorporation come with registration as an IPS. The society holds property and takes legal action in its own name. The assets of individual members are not put at risk if an IPS falls into debt.
- The rules and formalities are less rigid than under the Companies Acts.
- An IPS can convert into a limited company should it ever want to do so.
- It can be quick and relatively cheap to register if you are using model rules

submitted through a 'promoting society'. There are several 'promoting societies' which for a fee provide model rules, advice and help with registration for groups which fit their particular model. The Registry has available a full list of organisations that provide IPS model rules. The current fee for registering through one of the promoting societies is £140 (May 1986).

- Internal disputes can be referred to the Registrar of Friendly Societies for arbitration.

Disadvantages

- Loss of privacy. The society's rules and accounts are public.

- Time and expense if model rules are not adopted. The fee for registration without model rules is higher (£330 at May 1986) and there can be a delay in approving draft rules.

To sum up

The industrial and provident society could well be the legal structure you choose

- if you are seeking to become incorporated
- if your organisation is
  o a consumer or producer co-operative providing anything from building repairs to information and advice services.

3 Charitable Status

The legal structure of a voluntary group does not determine whether or not it can be a charity: charities may exist in all the constitutional forms discussed above.

It is important, however, to decide at the outset whether charitable status is to be sought since the contents of the governing instrument– in particular the objects clause setting out the aims of the organisation– will largely determine whether or not the group is capable of being a charity.

How to become a charity

In order to be accepted as a charity, you must first ensure that your group's purpose – as expressed in its governing instrument– is of a nature recognised as charitable within the law.

The next step will be to obtain recognition of this charitable status.

What does the law regard as charitable?

The concept of a charity is an old one and because English law has developed over the centuries, there is no simple, comprehensive definition of charity.

To be a charity an organisation

- must be exclusively charitable, i.e. *all* and not just some of its objects must be recognised by the law as charitable (NB this refers to the *objects* of the group. *Powers* exercised in furtherance of those objects and ancillary to them, e.g. raising money, owning property etc. need not be)
- must be for the benefit of the public or an appreciable section of the public, i.e. it should not be merely for the benefit of a particular group of private persons (but see relief of poverty below)

The law classifies charities under four heads:

- *Relief of poverty.* 'Poverty' is generously interpreted: it includes 'going short' as well as destitution.

  Exceptionally, organisations established for the relief of poverty are capable of being charities even if they provide benefit only to a limited group of people.

- *Advancement of education.* This can be broadly interpreted to include other kinds of education beside the three Rs. It does not include political propaganda, however, nor would the argument that all experience is educational be accepted by the courts or the Charity Commissioners.
- *Advancement of religion.* This is not limited to Christianity but must involve a belief in a deity.
- *Other purposes beneficial to the community.* It is under this head that the law can – and in practice does – extend the categories of organisations accepted as charities.

Charities whose objects are recreational fall under this category. They have been given statutory recognition in the Recreational Charities Act 1958, which extends the definition of charity to cover provision of facilities for recreation or other leisure-time occupation if the facilities are provided in the interests of social welfare.

It is unwise to rely on the category of 'other purposes beneficial to the community' as a catch-all category.

Legal advice will certainly be necessary if your group is seeking to establish as charitable any object that has not been previously accepted as such by the courts or the Charity Commissioners.

Recognition of charitable status: registration under the Charities Act 1960

To obtain the advantages of charitable status it is necessary to be recognised as a charity. The most obvious way of achieving this is to register with the Charity Commissioners, for once a charity has been registered it is presumed conclusively to be a charity for all practical purposes.

Charities are obliged to register unless they fall within an exempt group or are expressly excepted by order or statute. The exempt group includes friendly societies, other societies registered under the Friendly Societies Act, and industrial and provident societies, all of which are obliged to register with the Registrar of Friendly Societies (see above).

The excepted group embraces many smaller charities who are freed from the obligation to register if they have

- no permanent endowment (i.e. all property is expendable without distinction between capital and income)
- no income from property exceeding £15 a year
- no use and occupation of land

Even if your group is not obliged to register, it may still request registration and is strongly advised to do so.

If, therefore, your group intends to become a charity it should first send a copy of the draft governing instrument (in duplicate) to the Charity Commission (who in most cases call for details of the group's activities).

If the draft is not acceptable, it may be feasible at this stage to modify the objects expressed in the governing instrument and also the group's activities to meet the Commission's requirements.

Your group may be able to take advantage of a model document tailored to your kind of charity. The Charity Commission has a list of organisations which produce model governing instruments acceptable to them. (See also the appendix to this guide.)

Exceptionally, if your group intends to seek tax advantages as a charity without registration with the Charity Commission, it may send a draft copy of its governing instrument to the Charities Division of the Inland Revenue to see if it is acceptable to them before it is finally drawn up. This applies equally to organisations registered with the Registrar of Friendly Societies.

The advantages of charitable status

- Substantial financial privileges including
  - exemption from most forms of direct taxation, i.e. income tax, corporation tax and capital gains tax, providing the

income or gains are applied to charitable purposes only, and from capital transfer tax

o no generally privileged position in respect of VAT, but if a charity is registered for VAT (because it carries on business in excess of £20,500), certain supplies made *by* it will be zero-rated by reason of its charitable status; also certain supplies on which VAT is charged will be zero-rated if supplied *to* a charity. The latter will be of advantage to a charity which is not registered for VAT

o total exemption from stamp duty on conveyances and transfer of property to a charity

o relief of 50 per cent on local authority rates (and up to 100 per cent at the local authority's discretion) on property occupied by a charity and 'wholly or mainly' used for charitable purposes

o recovery of income tax on covenants made to a charity for a period of more than three years

• Privileged position when undertaking some forms of fund raising, e.g. small lotteries

• Good public image

• Eligibility for help, particularly financial, from other charities

The disadvantages of charitable status

• All of the objects of a charity must be charitable. If some of the proposed objects of a group are not charitable, it may be necessary to establish two separate organisations – one charitable and the other not – rather than losing the benefits of charitable status altogether. *Example*. A charity intends to trade on a substantial basis. A separate organisation (non-charitable) is set up with the result that the activities of the charity remain exclusively charitable and its income continues to be applied solely for charitable purposes. The profits from the trading group are covenanted to the charity which can recover the tax paid on them.

• Charitable status may restrict the group's political activity. Political activity – although not in itself charitable – is permissible within certain limits where it is in furtherance of the main charitable object. (See the guidelines issued by the Charity Commissioners which deal with this issue.) Nevertheless, the restrictions imposed by the limits may be a substantial reason for an organisation not to seek charitable status.

If political activity is contemplated by the group it may be necessary to seek legal advice from a solicitor or from the Charity Commission to see whether a choice will have to be made between such activity and charitable status.

• The Charity Commission has controlling and supervisory powers.

• Charitable status involves restrictions on altering the objects and on disposal of property on dissolution.

The Charity Commission

The Charity Commission has the general function of

'promoting the effective use of charitable resources by encouraging the development of better methods of administration by giving charity trustees information or advice on any matter affecting the charity and by investigating and checking abuses' (Charities Act 1960, s. 1(4)).

The supervisory and controlling functions of the Charity Commission should not be emphasised at the expense of its ability to assist in the following ways:

• It gives free advice on all charity matters. It can refer your group to relevant bodies when dealing with technical matters.

• Of particular value is the right of a single charity trustee (see below) to apply to the Commission for legal advice on any matter affecting his/her duty as a trustee.

If he/she acts in accordance with this advice he/she will be exonerated from what may subsequently prove to be a breach of trust.

- The Charity Commission establishes and maintains the register of charities, and receives accounts from charities.

It also provides the following services:

- *Charities Official Investment Scheme* which can enable small charities to receive the benefit of a broader spectrum of investment than would be available if they were the sole investor
- *The Official Custodian for Charities.* This officer operates as a holding trustee for charities. He can hold property on behalf of the charity and remit any income to it free of income tax. Because his office has no natural life span, he can continue to hold the property indefinitely avoiding the otherwise recurrent trouble and expense of conveying the property to new trustees.
- The Charity Commission can carry out steps for a charity that have become necessary, but are beyond the legal powers of the charity trustees (e.g. the removal and appointment of trustees, or the transfer of property).
- It can also in certain exceptional circumstances establish a scheme altering the terms of a charity's governing instrument.

Charity trustees

The term 'charity trustees' can confuse. 'Charity trustees' are defined in the Charities Act 1960 as 'those persons having the general control and management of the administration of a charity'.

Your charity may not appear to have trustees in the usual sense if its legal structure is not a trust; or there may only be holding trustees with no managerial functions (see above).

But a charity will always have 'charity' trustees even if they are not referred to as such. The charity trustees are the members of the management committee of an unincorporated association, the trustees of a trust and the directors of a company, i.e. in each case the people who run the charity. They are called 'trustees' because the law imposes upon each of them the responsibilities of trustees. These include the following:

- A charity trustee must know the contents of the governing instrument, in particular the objects of the charity and the means by which they may be carried out. Any departure from its terms will be a breach of trust and render the trustees personally liable to make good any loss to the charity.

  There is, however, provision for the court to relieve a trustee from personal liability where he or she has acted honestly and reasonably and ought fairly to be excused for a breach of trust.
- A charity trustee must take as much care in any dealings carried out on behalf of the charity as would a prudent person in handling his or her own affairs.
- A charity trustee must see that proper accounts are kept. If the charity is registered, it must submit to the Charity Commissioners such accounts as they require.
- Charity trustees should act jointly. Each major decision must be considered by the whole body of trustees or if the governing instrument requires only a quorum, by that quorum representing the whole body of trustees.

  It is not sufficient for the charity trustees to delegate the making of a decision to one of their number or to a professional adviser, although of course they may seek advice before reaching a decision.

  Once they have considered a matter, however, they do not have to be unanimous but unlike other trustees may act by majority decision.

  It is essential for charity trustees to keep minutes, particularly if a dissenting minority wishes to dissociate themselves from any action taken.

- A charity trustee must not profit from the trust. This rule must be strictly observed. It extends to a prohibition on purchasing charity property even at a fair price, or supplying goods to a charity.

If you are engaged with others in running a charity, it is important that you are aware of your position and obligations as a trustee. Nevertheless this should not inhibit you from taking such a position.

The Charity Commission will advise even a single charity trustee on any matter affecting the performance of his or her duty. Where this advice is acted upon the trustee will be protected from any subsequent charge of breach of trust.

4 Postscript by Adrian Longley

As the preceding pages have amply shown, those starting a voluntary group are faced with a bewildering variety of constitutions to choose from. A glance at the chapter headings alone may be intimidating, so that readers who have travelled thus far are to be congratulated. But has the journey really been worthwhile?

I believe it has, for a number of reasons. Initially, when hopes are high and all the founding members are working amicably together towards a common end, a formal constitution may well be seen as a bureaucratic obstacle, an unnecessary piece of red tape. Often it is only when enthusiasm wanes and differences arise that its usefulness can be perceived. No document will cover every eventuality. But if, after careful thought, one of the forms recommended in the text is adopted, the promoters will find they have avoided many of the common causes of friction: rights and duties of members, frequency of meetings, alterations to meet changed circumstances, disposal of assets on winding up – to name but a few. Above all, two crucial questions will have been clarified: who is to exercise ultimate control, and is any special status – in particular, charity status – desired and/or feasible?

Whatever the nature of the enterprise, time spent on choosing the right kind of constitution is never wasted.

Adrian Longley

Appendix

Organisations offering model or specimen governing instruments

A model can be adopted in its entirety. A specimen can be adapted to meet individual requirements. Unlike a model, it never declares specific objects.

Civic Trust
17 Carlton House Terrace
London SW1Y 5AW
Tel. 01-930 0914
Publishes a model constitution for a local amenity society.

Co-operative Development Agency
Broadmead House
21 Panton Street
London SW1Y 4DR
Tel. 01-839 2988
Produces model rules for worker co-operatives, neighbourhood co-operatives and community co-operatives.

Councils for Voluntary Service – National Association
26 Bedford Square
London WC1B 3HU
Tel. 01-636 4066
Produces a model constitution for councils for voluntary service.

Industrial Common Ownership Movement (ICOM)
The Corn Exchange
Leeds LS1 7BP
Tel. 0532-461736/8
Produces a model memorandum and articles of association for a company limited by guarantee (non-charitable) and 'How to start an industrial co-op', a kit which includes model rules, forms for registration as an IPS and guidance on procedure.

Job Ownership Ltd (JOL)
9 Poland Street
London W1V 3DG
Tel. 01-437 5511
Produces a model for a co-operative company limited by shares based on 'Mondragon' principles.

16

London Adventure Playground Association
28 Underwood Road
London E1 5AW
Tel. 01-377 0314
Publishes a model constitution for an adventure playground group.

National Confederation of Parent-Teacher Associations
43 Stonebridge Road
Northfleet
Gravesend
Kent DA11 9DS
Tel. 0474-60618
Produces a model constitution for a PTA.

National Council for Voluntary Organisations
26 Bedford Square
London WC1B 3HU
Tel. 01-636 4066

Publishes a specimen constitution for an unincorporated organisation having a membership; a specimen deed for a charitable trust; a model trust deed for a village hall; and a specimen memorandum and articles of association for a charitable company limited by guarantee.

National Federation of Community Organisations
8/9 Upper Street
London N1 0PQ
Tel. 01-226 0189
Produces a model constitution for a community association.

Pre-school Playgroups Association
61–63 Kings Cross Road
London WC1X 9LL
Tel. 01-833 0991
Publishes a model constitution for a local group.

further Reading

Charity Commission.
'Political Activities by Charities'. *Report of the Charity Commissioners for England and Wales for the year 1981*, HMSO. 'Commissioners Decisions and Opinions on Charitable Status: The Promotion of Racial Harmony', *Report of the Charity Commissioners for England and Wales for the year 1983*, HMSO, pp. 9–11. (The Charity Commissioners produce a range of free leaflets on various aspects of charity law and charitable activities.)

Companies Registration Office. 'Incorporation of New Companies (notes for guidance): Notes for the Guidance of Registered Companies', Companies Registration Office, Crown Way, Mairdy, Cardiff CF4 3UZ.

Cracknell, D. G. *Law Relating to Charities*, Oyez Longman, 2nd edn, 1983.

Elliott, M. and Smith, P. *Little Women: how to start a home care co-operative*, Community Service Volunteers, 1985, 24pp. (contains specimen constitutions).

Hansen, O. 'Community Organisations: forming a common ownership enterprise: Part 1. Co-operative and common ownership principles', *Legal Action Group Bulletin*, Nov. 1981, pp. 256–61.

Liverpool City Solicitors Department Community Liaison Section, 'How to compile, adopt and use a constitution, guide notes for community organisations', Liverpool City Solicitors Department, undated.

London Voluntary Service Council, *Voluntary but not Amateur: a guide to the law for voluntary organisations and community groups*, LVSC, 1981.

Luyster, C. *The New Co-operatives: a directory and resource guide* 4th edn, Co-operative Development Agency, 1986.

Milton Keynes Community Bookshop. *The Companies Act 1948–1981: A company limited by guarantee and not having a share capital: memorandum and articles of association of Milton Keynes Community Bookshop*, Milton Keynes Community Bookshop, 1982, 11pp.

National Council for Voluntary Organisations.
What is a Charity? Charity Law and Formation of Charities (Information Sheet No. 20), NCVO, 1986.
Charities: Constitutional Forms and Liabilities of Trustees (Guidance Note 2), NCVO, 1981.
Legal Responsibilities of Members of Committees of Unincorporated Voluntary Organisations (Guidance Note 1), NCVO, 1981.

National Federation of Community Organisations. *Charitable Status and Registration*, NFCO, 1983, 5pp.

Phillips, A. and Smith, K. *Charitable Status: a practical handbook*, Inter-Action Imprint, 2nd edn, 1982.

Scarman, Lord. *The Powers and Duties of Trustees*, 23rd report of the Law Reform Committee, HMSO, 1982, Cmnd. 8733, 72pp.

Sheridan, L. A. and Keeton, G. *Modern Law of Charities*, University College Cardiff Press, 3rd edition, 1983, 502pp.

Underhill, M. *The Licensing Guide*, Oyez Longman, 1982, 8th edition, 117pp.

Voluntary Action Westminster. *Organisational Structure and Charitable Status*, Voluntary Action Westminster, 1982, 4pp.

Wales Council for Voluntary Action. *Constitutions* (WCVA Information Sheet No. 2), 1983, 5pp.